The Letter Critters

Illustrated and Written by Chase Taylor

I dedicate this book to my loving family.

About the Author

Chase Taylor is seventeen years old and he lives with autism. He LOVES letters. Since he was a little boy, he had a passion for letters. Chase struggles with being social but is willing to share his letter characters with the world. This is Chase's first book publication. All proceeds will be donated to a non-profit autism organization.

About this Book

This book will encourage children to learn letters by looking at these cute illustrations. It will show kids what the letters look like and what begins with those letters.

A is afraid of ants.

B likes big blue balloons.

C is very cold.

D is a dynamic doctor.

E has enormous ears.

F has feathers and can fly.

G likes to play his guitar.

H is in hazardous heat.

I is icky and has ideas.

J jumps for joy.

K likes to kick her ball.

L loves lemonade.

M munches his meal.

N is negative and nasty.

O loves to sing opera.

P likes to eat popcorn.

Q has a quacking quacker.

R likes to ride race cars.

S likes slithery snakes.

T likes to tap dance.

U is under her umbrella.

V is victorious.

W is a wicked winker.

X is X-traordinary.

Y yells for you.

Z zips and zooms.